SUGAR ZONE

OTHER BOOKS BY MARY MACKEY

Poetry

Breaking The Fever, Marsh Hawk Press
The Dear Dance of Eros, Fjord Press
Skin Deep, Gallimaufry Press
One Night Stand, Effie's Press
Split Ends, Ariel Press

Novels

The Widow's War, Berkley Books
The Notorious Mrs. Winston, Berkley Books
The Year The Horses Came, Harper San Francisco
The Horses At the Gate, Harper San Francisco
The Fires of Spring, Penguin
Season of Shadows, Bantam
The Kindness of Strangers, Simon & Schuster
A Grand Passion, Simon & Schuster
The Last Warrior Queen, Putman
McCarthy's List, Doubleday
Immersion, Shameless Hussy Press

SUGAR ZONE

poems

Mary Mackey

M
H
P

Marsh Hawk Press
East Rockaway, NY • 2011

11 12 13 14 15   7 6 5 4 3 2 1   First Edition

Marsh Hawk Press books are published by Poetry Mailing List, Inc., a not-for-profit corporation under section 501 (c) 3 United States Internal Revenue Code.

Cover and author photos by Angus Wright.
Cover and interior design by Claudia Carlson.
The text and display are set in Bembo and Bembo Book.

Library of Congress Cataloging-in-Publication Data

Mackey, Mary.
Sugar zone : poems / by Mary Mackey.
p. cm.
ISBN-13: 978-0-9846353-1-3 (pbk.)
ISBN-10: 0-9846353-1-9 (pbk.)
I. Title.
PS3563.A3165S84 2011
811'.54--dc22

2011012824

Marsh Hawk Press
P.O. Box 206, East Rockaway, N.Y. 11518-0206
www.marshhawkpress.org

for A.W.

Acknowledgments

I would like to thank Dr. Lise Sedrez, Professor of Latin American History at California State University, Long Beach. Dr. Sedrez, born and reared in Rio de Janeiro, patiently and expertly proofread all the Portuguese words and phrases in this collection. Sandy McIntosh, Jane Augustine, and Thomas Fink's editorial suggestions were invaluable, as were those of the members of the Entrekin poetry group. Dorothy Hearst, Elizabeth Stark, and Pamela Berkman gave me companionship during the creation of these poems as did the women of Word Of Mouth Bay Area and the staff and Fellows of the Virginia Center for the Creative Arts. Lastly, I want to thank my husband Angus Wright for sharing his expertise in Brazilian history and for his unfailing affection and support.

Some of these poems were previously published in the following magazines and anthologies:

Omnidawn Press Blog
Mad Hatter's Review
Rufous City Review
Marsh Hawk Review

Preface

Although many poems in this collection contain Portuguese words and phrases, the English-only portions are complete poems in themselves. They stand alone and can be read as if they were written solely in English. On the other hand, Portuguese speakers will find subtle levels of meaning contained in the Portuguese phrases which enhance and deepen the poems. This Interlingual collection attempts to weave two remarkably rich languages together into poetry that is seamless, musical, and global.

Contents

PART I

SUGAR

1. The Jaguars
That Prowl Our Dreams

The Jaguars That Prowl Our Dreams

Up on the Orinoco, Rio Negro, Solimões,
Tocantins, Xingu, Javary
they're drinking the *bebida preta*/black drink
snake vine ayahuasca/yage/   blood of the great anaconda
with the smoke of burning rainforests in their nostrils
and *o gosto de cinzas*/taste of ashes on their tongues

Eles estão comendo   they're eating
purple snails   powdered viper venom
lagartas esmagadas   flowers that dye their lips
the color of blood   singing of cities of blue glass
and the jaguars that prowl our dreams

O que mais/what else   are they seeing?
O que mais/what else   do they know?

they're not saying
they're not telling
they're calling on the ghost tribes instead

ghosts of the *Tupinambá, Tupiniquim, Aimoré*
lost upriver forever
lost in the burning world

A Visitor's Guide to the Favelas of Rio

Rocinha, Mangueira, Morro de Macacos
up on the hills they are casting the shells
Um coro de vozes femininas cantando
looking into the future   rattling the *búzios*
pasting dyed chicken feathers on Carnival floats
beheading dogs smoking crack   burning
the buses   *não esperam a noite*

in Cantagalo, Serrinha, Salguiero
they are calling on Xangô the warrior   Exu
who opens and closes roads   Oshun who eats
acarajé cooked with palm oil thick as sewage
orange as longing

here on the beach the waves rush toward us
bruising our legs and sucking us in
cuidado   beware of the undertow

Babilônia, Cajueiro, Tavares Bastos
Morro Azul, Jacarezinho, Cidade de Deus
gunfire rattles off the cinderblock houses
there are dead roses in the water
gold-wrapped candy   papayas   gum

who made these offerings?
what gods do they pray to?
when will we meet them?
what will they want?

Dreaming of the Bullet-Proof Cars of Maceió

This is the *terra do açúcar e maus sonhos*
the land of sugar and bad dreams
infinite darkness without borders
where birds passing overhead
smell like *biscoitos molhados*/wet crackers
sour milk and the sweat of sex
aqui/here in the night room   doorknobs turn
your hands   mirrors reflect receding galaxies
and the clown who lies on his back beside you
twitching and suffering   is your soul

wake up   *acordar!*   tell me why nothing moves
why starving people lean into their shadows
like flies caught in amber
why the past goes on eating the present
like a rising ocean eats the beach

tell me why they are burning
palm trees on the road to the airport
why the water tastes like ashes
why the windows of the cars are blind

at low tide the children drink cachaça
and call on Iemanjá   fishtailed mother of storms
wake up and tell me why the sand beneath this city
keeps shifting   why all the stores are stocked with
hallucinations   tell me why Solange left
and where she went

Sugar Zone

Sempre me amedrontou   I have always
been afraid   tankers strung out along the horizon
like a necklace of black
seeds   a *idéia de ter um filho*   of the idea
of having a child   let's get drunk
on *cachaça* forget her outstretched
hands her face   the delicate angle of her nose
her children selling candy roses   *cor de pedras*
color of stones amethyst, emerald, diamond
all day the tankers come and go   the mill grinds
barefoot men and women cut
and cut

for a whole week I missed Solange
Por uma semana eu tive saudade
then clarity for three days
limpeza   *limpeza*
they sleep on the
black and white tiles that wind beneath our feet
steal the food off our plates
We eat behind fences
the ticks drop off the
trees and settle between our cold beer
and cashews   plastic straws blow down the beach
like transparent wands   *a cidade só voltara a existir*
depois de 20 de janeiro   (this city has only existed
since the 20th of January)   for twenty minutes I
stood in the deserted street
  fiquei olhando/looking
for something
          no longer
there

This is a Poem Creating Itself

Este é um poema criando-se
this is a poem creating itself *em um idioma*
in a language you don't understand

think of it as a dancer
whose face is hidden behind a beaded veil
uma bebida preta   a black drink that
lets you hear jaguars speak
a city seen from 20,000 feet
um barulho/ a noise that wakes you *à meia-noite*
tropeçando tropeçando   stumbling through the
darkness   knocking at your door

Discussing Catastrophe

Up on the hill in the white villa
with its carved stairs and Moorish windows
we are sitting on wrought iron chairs discussing catastrophe
how the earth shook the volcano erupted
the hurricane blew in the plague swept through
leaving stones like rows of articulated bones

our sweet drinks are bitter
we suck limes and cherries and taste
dust moldy cardboard the acrid backwash
of burned flesh

the sun is scorching the horizon tipping the knife
blade line of clouds with arterial red some
think we should send money or go down to the city
and dig through the rubble with our bare hands
the rest of us just want to admire the view

to our left the ocean is turning black
above the slate-like calm a funnel of pelicans slowly rises
over the unsuspecting fish

The Drowning Boys

Down to the Farol do Barra on the Bay of All Saints
out to the raw sugar beaches of Jaguaribe and Itapuã
stomachs empty as charity
bare feet coated with salt and the mud of melted hills
Eles estão chegando   here they come
the drowning boys/*as moleques da rua*
from Susuranna, Favela de Alagados,
Maciel/Pelourinho   coming in packs
like dancing saints   their faces bright as the mirror
Iemanjá holds when she walks on the waves

as crianças sem esperança   the boys without hope

how gently they will touch our wrists
as they unstrap our watches
how carefully they will turn us over
as they empty our pockets & push us under

these children who don't fear death
children who   in another life
we might have loved

Conquistadors

Until the fall of the first rains
we possess nothing but hope
the streets of this lost city
are tracks of black salt
spilled on a table
wounded dancers weaving drunkenly
past sleeping dogs

at night we dream of high cliffs
studded with crystals
tunnels that lead to palms
and water

the heat is a long hiss
a desert of bones
a hawk circling over an endless
hallucination

long ago we rode here
looking for gold
now we long for things
we don't deserve
water that does not burn our throats
sleep that does not bring madness
long nights   gray clouds   cold sand

Obituary for a City That Is Still Alive

Cidade da noite/cidade em chamas   *city of night/city on fire*
cidade de ossos/cidade de segredos   *city of bones/city of secrets*

—Cléa Abreu

It's the small things we'll remember later
not the great buildings stuck in rows like ice
trays or the men in black suits swarming
the sidewalks like army ants   but a bare maple
strung between anticipation and a sky so clear
it looks like glass   the sweet taste of chestnuts
the feeling of mashing them against the roof of our mouth

a little girl in a red jacket dashing
across a playground to kick a blue ball
three pigeons on a wire
a fruit stand stocked with green grapes
the head of a sunflower spiraling down the gutter
the sound our shoes make on wet concrete   the way our shadows
shrink when we turn toward the light

when we close our eyes, we'll see the faces of strangers
opening and folding like multicolored fans
and in our ears (which long ago went deaf to hope)
we will hear their voices whispering   *nada*
nichivo   *nadinha*   *nothing*

Walking Upside Down on the Other Side of the World

Quando falamos nesta cidade perdida
when we speak in this lost city
our words bubble out of our mouths
like the *orações*/prayers of drowned children
through air so hot and green   it holds us
in suspension like bottled glass

here *perto deste grande rio*/near this great river
on the edge of this great forest of stumps
anaconda clouds glide over us like sinuous birds
and the throats of lovers fill with mud and black water

here you can get anyone killed for $50
by the *jagunços* in cowboy boots and aviator glasses
who sit in the bars nursing cold beers

here iron ore is sucked out of
the earth like blood   and a section
of bamboo filled with
gold dust will buy a you a quick death

in this Anopheles democracy of sudden disasters
mosquitoes spread malaria equally to everyone
garimpeiros, caboclos, assassins,
colonels who ride in air conditioned cars
babies who sleep in hammocks

here the dead speak the words
the living are afraid to utter
and each kiss   given in fear
is as swift as the tongue of a bat
probing a flower

Solange

Solange wants something white
(*uma coisa branca*)   a shard of bone
a broken cup   something (*de carne, de luz)*
that steams like dry ice   burns her lips
flays the palms of her hands   sends her dancing
across a plain of broken glass
    she wants it to fall suddenly (*de repente*)
out of a white sky   turn her hair into a torch
strip the trees   blind the birds

Raptor/Falcão

in the hot lands   *nas terras tórridas*   the Milky Way hovers
over us like a great white osprey

falcão/falcão

waiting with infinite patience
wings outspread   golden irises masked
with a membrane blue as *água*
amanhecer   *morte*   dawn

star/hawk gliding from east
to west   *subindo/descendo*

rising/falling

first the silence
then the terror
then the slow implacable
descent

Epidemic

Quando os teus olhos fecharem	*When your eyes close*
E as tuas mãos repousarem	*And your hands rest*
No peito frio e deserto,	*On the cold desert of your chest*
Hão de morrer as cantigas.	*Your songs have to die*
	—Joaquim Cardozo

I wake in a strange room
in a strange country
where the petals of the flowers
are razor blades and the ground is
glue

outside my window two suns are
copulating   throwing shadows
that scald like acid

after a while (or a second/or perhaps
never)   two strangers appear
and demand that I tell them my name

but I no longer know
who I am

they say they want to show me
ice   cold mountains   the mouths
of the dead

I imagine a small space opening
between two lips   a cup filled
with small, gray birds   medicines
that cure everything

when I lift my hands
I discover I can see through them
my tongue tastes like wet wool

my chest is filled with sand
under my nails I see deep canyons
bottomed with black water and a thin
rim of something green that
smells like fennel

Santa Marta to Bogota

they are burning the fields

as the train moves through the ashes
you put   your arms around me
to keep me from stepping off
into the nothingness   on the other
side of the rail

above us the stars   float
grimy and abandoned
as cinders

    what do you want to do with your life?
you ask
    who do you want to be?

no one
everything
I say

(there is soot under my nails   soot on my tongue
soot in my mouth

where have we been?
where are we going?
why the fuck do you interrogate me?)

Somewhere Nowhere

Eu sonho   I dream that *meu*
cérebro   my brain   is a forest
denso/verde   dense/green   branched
trembling in the wind
of each heartbeat

when I wake I see a red
sunset blossoming upside down
reversões, reversões   outside
in a city I don't recognize
the traffic drones like locusts

tenho saudades de Solange
I miss Solange
her *olhos do largato*
her lizard eyes
Solange who knows what it is
to be muted by pain

diga-me o que aconteceu
tell me what happened

quando Solange abrirá seus dedos bem abertos
when Solange spread her fingers
the shadow of her hand
was like a sheet of molten glass

diga-me onde estou   tell me
where I am
where she   is

tell me if you can
where suffering   breaks off
from speech

2. Latitude Zero

There's No Sin South of the Equator

Pull back the covers   turn off the lights
let's get high on *pango, liamba, dirijo, birra,*
elva, fininha, fumo de Angola

at sixty degrees south cyclonic winds
swirl around the pole without ceasing
nothing stops them   not land   not remorse
not confession
nada

right now   under our bed
icebergs are being tossed like scree
by waves that carry the bones and wrecks
and broken masts of every part of us that ever went
down

below the equator
sin does not exist
but we have learned this too late

venha   come
enter the great emptiness
that encircles the world
see *the história infeliz*
the sad   history
love has ordained

Cali

do you remember how the light from the streetlamps
coated us like brown glass   how we lay
listening to the whir of the fan   the whine of mosquitoes
a bottle breaking in the street below
machinegun fire   screams   tanks rumbling past

something flared pink and orange
extravagant as a silk scarf and a chip
of cement flew over us and buried itself
in the wall half an inch from
your head

we rolled to the floor   crawled
to the bathroom   took refuge
in the shower   turned on the water
and held each other laughing
as if being together made us immortal

all night death drew shadows
on the walls   the water coiled
down the drain in the wrong direction
once I looked up and saw something
calm and terrible in your face
as if you had always known
this would happen   as if you
welcomed it

Along the River

along the river *morro de saudade*
morro de saudade e paixão

I am dying of longing
dying of longing and passion
the trees are rusting

morro de saudade
não penso em outra coisa
I can't think of anything else
and the water is already   winter-black

se eu colocar minha mão
if I put in my hand
I am afraid I will draw back something   cold
something clear
something that will shatter like glass

The Kama Sutra of Kindness: Position Number 4

you claim you long for me   the way
a drowning man longs to breathe

poised above me   tortured as a saint
you pause then descend   speaking
with a tongue that tastes of honey
and salt

reason be damned

look
even the light around has
changed

The Kama Sutra of Kindness: Position Number 5

in the flame
of a single candle   entire cities
    are appearing
    and disappearing

my hands tremble on you
my fingers pass through you
your tongue tastes like apples
your flesh is fog

above our roof   the jealous moon
has torn a hole in the sky

On a Sea of Burning Roses

Sobre um mar de rosas que arde

— Pedro Kilkerry

we float on a sea of burning roses
overhead the sky is slowly
drooping like a great lilac
pelting us with petals
that smell like cloves

back on the beach
they are preparing to save us

but I don't want
to be saved

Medusa

above us wrapped in carpet thick air
the grand hotel that drugs built   ice black
cars   boys with teeth like sharks   machine
guns   dry hills   stray goats   a dead pelican

below our bodies folded between the creases of the waves
jellyfish   *água-viva* charged with neurotoxins
each sting bringing a flash of blue light
each opening a door

Huichol paintings snake across the insides
of our eyelids   gods with heads like great pink
eggs   triangular stars hammering at the sky
severed fingers   orange jaguars   nameless things
that revolve searing us from head to toe

Medusa shakes out her long curls and floats toward
us pulsing and trembling   a magenta globe delicate
as a soap bubble   wrapping her tentacles around our
legs   she cradles us in pain so intense it verges on
ecstasy

as we float here   between two deaths
something is burning   something bleeding
something going numb   something
going down

You Are a Part of Me I Once Inhabited

a house with large rooms   and outside the windows
a pond of silver fish floating in the shadows
and a flowering vine   perhaps a rose

over all our green lawn   white things drifted
with transparent wings or petals shaped like stars

there was light everywhere
and the kind of silence that made us feel
as if our ears had been stopped
with wax

when we breathed   the house breathed with us
and the smoke from our chimney
rose without wavering

all day we fought and suffered
and threatened to abandon each other

all night we slept hand in hand

Bone China

Eu canto porque   I sing because
o instante existe   the instant exists
in the cup you forgot to wash   the cup
you threw into the sink   in the tea leaves
that keep forming and reforming into flowers
pencils and the faces of those I've loved

eu canto/I sing because you forgot to wash the cup
because in it I can smell jasmine, sex
the cast-off skins of snakes

time is a pet that slithers at our feet
black and gold and fanged   *então eu canto*
and so I sing   *não sou alegre nem triste*
not happy or sad   as *atrás*/behind us
something fades   and before us
something flowers

The High, Hard Mountains

The high, hard mountains write letter by letter
the story of how we met in a dense
forest   on a deer trail   in a column of light
charged with dust and pollen

the wind rose
shadows rushed across your face
like flocks of small birds
taking flight

you said something to me
  something urgent
(perhaps you warned me)

but I had gone deaf   I saw your lips moving
but I could not (did not want to)
read them

What Wind What Horse What Terrible Longing

Que vento, que cavalo, que bravía
saudade me arrastava a esse deserto,
me obrigava a adorar o que sofria?

—Cecília Meirelles

What wind   what horse   what terrible
longing compels me to cross this desert
forces me to suffer and adore my suffering?

I could sleep two inches from you
and never touch you
raise my hand over your face
and never let it fall

inhale the smallest portion
of your breath
and leave the rest for you

I could stand by and watch you take
other lovers and be glad
though I burned with jealousy
and wept with despair

you will not give me
  your foot
  your stocking
  or even your shoe

leave me your footprint
so I can rest my hand in it
and feel your absence

Latitude Zero

the temptation to follow pushes us forward
like a strong wind   when we flee
before a storm

when did we first see   mud-sopped rivers
littered with hammock-strung boats   cathedrals of sunken
trees circled by *botos rosas* and neon-striped fish

the treasures that float up from the bottom
are always *elétrica*   carnivorous
impossible to abandon

so we have spent our lives
swimming after lost things   *o cheiro de almas*
cidades perdidas   foods we can no longer buy at any price
raw sugar   foreign gods

3. The Cold Lands

Walking in Two Worlds

On the border between *sonho e silêncio*/dream and silence
Something crouches in the rugs
rustles in the china cabinet   whispers in
the tables and chairs

only a thickness
in the air   only a quick movement
caught out of the corner of one eye
something from the jungles of the south
a cloud of white termites   the scent
of catuaba   shadows that tremble incessantly

Xangô god of thunder   Olokun owner of oceans
here in the cold lands
the paperweights on the windowsills
are starting fires
aqui nas terras frígidas
the snow is burning

here   something
is following at our heals
hunting us down   taking our measure
unweaving our dreams

Yansan

strums the bare trees
plays the piano key pyramid steps
river ice cracking
snake strings crawling
feet stamping packed earth

plays something being sacrificed
something being born
plays breath in
breath out
breath of the tornado
sweeping out of a green glass sky
breath of the whisper you hide in your lover's ear

Yansan plays the wind   the silent
rapture of fog   and always behind her you can hear
that back-up girl group twang of limbs
singing along   beating against one another
like a thousand rushing hearts

In the Cold Lands

Here in the cold lands/*nas terras frígidas*   the fog
slides into our dreams   *nada tem uma cor brilhante*
no macaws, mangos, *onças-pintadas,* palm trees swaying
like carnival dancers

here the monsters of despair come every night   Beowulf
gripping the bloody head of Grendel's mother   seafarers who
measure their years in winters   women who have no names
given to strangers as peace offerings   wild seas
that crush the hulls of ships

here the days are short as broken sticks   and the drowned
freeze rightside up with their eyes open   *Iemanjá, Obá, Ogun,*
Xangô   *onde ficam*/where are   the trances of the south
the ceremonies   the *Mães de Santos*

when we bow our heads to pray   the wind is a blade
and such gods as there are   /   are indifferent as
skinning knives

Emergency Supplies

the disaster we plan for is never
the disaster that happens

stock wood and matches   & it floods
boats   & everything burns

catastrophe comes randomly   like a great crow
working its way along a horizon of sticks
snapping one here
                        one there
but never the one you expect

All the Way Down

the car fell very   slowly
turning like a wheel
of light

inside   we lost
all power to think
swam in midair all the way down
without remembering
the rocks that lay below

clear as water   minds purified
of terror
how easily we breathed in
this new element
how serenely   we stared
out the windows

near the end we saw
great waving fans of coral
and schools of silver fish
no bigger than our thumbs

the music of whale songs
played incessantly in our ears
and briefly   (very briefly)
we were happy

Roadkill

I avert my eyes from the tortured metal
and burned plastic of your
life

at the end   a single
white foot, bare   another in a red
sock

the indignity
the rotten joke   of death

The Night You Never Saw

Indian women in huipiles bearing branches
of candied apples dipped in sugar dark as dried blood
families drinking mescal and glasses of scarlet
jacaranda juice / eating mole and quesadillas stuffed
with white cheese that drips out the sides like
rubber bands

you would have walked across that plaza (on that night
you never saw) and found in some dark alley   scuttled with rats
some teenage girl about to cut her wrists   some heroin
addict with a needle in his arm   some disappointed lover
already holding a gun to his head   and said

in that Spanish you took such pains to learn (and would
never use again)   *Vamos a regatear*/let's make a deal   *tu vida*/your
life   *por mi muerte*/for my death   your

sad/hopeless/tragic/terrible/ life that lets you see
this cheap tinseled ordinary night creating itself
from one instant to the next   like laughter   like joy

Hunting Season

this is what will take
us all sooner or later
something that comes
loping suddenly
out of a white fog
its hot breath on the back of our necks   a quick blow

a broken sky
the smell of a hunger so raw
it feels like love

Little Enough

the core of it was nothing

not a village burned   not
even a dragon fly   dead dry and
curled   you could not put the tip
of your tongue through it

smaller than a needle of glass
jammed into your foot
smaller than the first suggestion of
morning in midwinter   it had so little
duration   it wasn't even an icicle
or a row of shadows thrown on
a wall   that danced themselves
mad then vanished

you could not capture it in your mouth   or hand
or trap it under a jar

you could not inhale it   understand
it   but it was there   with tiny
claws and teeth so small and
sharp   you never felt them
clamp down

Cold Snap

dying is something you only do
once

you don't have to get good at it

Absolution

Spread your arms   drift
until death is so far away
it looks like a ragged ridge of mountains
blued with pine sap and desire

forget the multiplication tables
the date of the Norman Conquest
the smell of oranges and burned forests
bitter water   air that tastes like gravel and almonds

everything you did right is erased
everything wrong   undone

Counter Clockwise

Os segredos do norte the secrets of the north
são escritos/are written on glass
look up and see the soles of their shoes
look down and see a blue slaked ocean
and a dancing flame

enter/*entra* *nesta casa* this house
call out your mother's name
backwards run your fingers around
every drain *anti-horário*
left to right/widdershins

at dawn you will wake to find your
eyes full of blood then sleep and
dream of a great continent made
of gold beaten so thin
you can wrap it
   around your tongue

Se você pudesse ser

if you could be/ *tão tranquilo*   still as a tree
você veria /you would see   *as sementes caírem*
the seeds fall   the shoots *germinarem*/rise and dance
    thicken leaf stretch   *copular*/mate
in bursts of yellow pollen   *debaixo*
beneath   your feet *flores flores*   flowers
would pulse *vibrando vibrando* in quick
carpeted colors

este é o grande presente   this is the great
gift: to be outside of time   to see it
sweep by

PART II

DANCING FOR THE SOLDIERS

Dancing for the Soldiers

When I was 3 I danced
for the soldiers propped up
in their hospital beds   their boy faces
white as the blank movie
screen behind me

my shadow dancing there
tall as a giant

pinwheel girl
whirligig girl
the girl whose job has
always been to make you
forget

Uncle Wid's Wagon

In the morning Grandmother sends us out with the mail
standing side-by-side in the back of the truck
clutching the top of the cab
competing to see who can yell
the loudest   eating dust
that tastes like stale Necco Wafers   careening around
corners   attempting to fly
chipping our teeth on gravel

at the crossroads
by the general store where Great-grandfather Horace
Ebenezer once courted his fancy woman
Uncle Wid waits for us
accompanied by two mules
he loves more than Aunt Ebbie

thin as an old rooster,
hard as a fence post
a riverboat cook with a laugh you can hear
three counties over and enough lines
in his face to remap all
of Kentucky

when he finally stubs out his cigarette
with his thumb and slaps the reins
the mules baulk and we learn new words
bitch bastard   gee   haw

Come on y'ol sons of bitches! he yells
The mules flatten their ears against their heads
expose yellow teeth the size
of piano keys lunge forward and the wagon
starts up   creaking and rattling like a pair of lovers
flailing away in an unglued bed

we bounce down the road past the Cooks' place
(our sworn enemies since 1792)
past the family graveyard
with its infant burials and kawumpus stones
eyes stinging
faces bloodied with red dust

the day grows hotter
the corn glistens and trembles
breathing out secrets
it only tells
to children

this   all of this
is what the past takes
with it
when it packs up
and leaves

The Thing at the Crossroads

They say when the owl hit the shutter and fell
onto her breast   Aunt Fen rose at midnight
spinster-lean with spotted hands and
teeth the color of bones and buckeyes

all she intended to do was check on
the baby who lay in its cradle
so white and cold she often thought it was
dead   but instead (for no reason she could
ever articulate) she went out barefoot across
the soft dirt of the yard

the dust ran like satin beneath her
feet and the darkness was so thick
she felt as if she were breathing black silk
that night the corn in the bottom
lands looked like a field of flames and the water
in the river burned like molten lead

she walked on   and at the exact spot where
one road sliced through another she found it
waiting for her

when it reached out for her she stepped straight
through it and came out the other side changed in a
way she would never describe although she lived
seventy more years in that same house with the doors
latched and the shutters barred

Mother at 90

At 90 she remembers her life as a series
of dinner parties   tables set with crystal
and silver   lobsters cracked just so
barrels of oysters flown in from the East
wild rice   drawn butter   martinis
in glasses so cold they stuck to her fingers

how they smoked and laughed   all those
friends who come back to her now in dreams
floating unrooted like river weeds

She has always longed
for beauty and order   longed for it more
than love   white linen   obedient
children   a brick house with a widow's walk

once when she was young   she stepped
out into the night and an owl
flew past her   heavy   soft silent
swift   hunting for all the small frightened
things that live in darkness

My Father's Leaves

when he was very old
my father told me he had lost
his leaves

he held out his hands   thin
& cold & I
took them in mine & said   your
gloves   Daddy
you lost your gloves

and thus I tracked him
& loved him
through metaphor

Assembling a Husband from Ordinary Household Objects

Forget those sugar skulls
that snapped between your
teeth   those rubber ladders that flung
you face down in the dirt   the sound
of windows breaking   freight trains
squashing pennies   termites
seething beneath your feet

get up now   gather
tape, staples, glue
a colander   a putty knife a strip
of Velcro   consider the philodendron
the kitchen sponge   the dog's
tongue

You have everything you need
    if you can only
find it

Rapture

I have no tale to tell but tipsiness and rapture.

—Rumi

All it takes
is a child running
on a day
in mid-winter
through blue light
the snow falling
the wind sharp

for no reason
toward no goal
in that single   ecstatic
mid-winter moment
the sound of the child's
boot buckles flapping
each step crackling
like candy wrappers

far behind
ever farther
the windows of the house
grow purple and opaque

suddenly
the child stops
turns and spins
spins and turns
head back   mouth open
eyes closed

PART III

THE LAND OF BAD DREAMS

This Is the Land of Bad Dreams

This is the land of bad dreams
where birds passing overhead
smell like wet crackers and blood
sour milk and the sweat of sex
the night room   where doorknobs
turn your hands   and mirrors reflect
the clown that lies on his back
beside you   twitching suffering
reincarnated as a castrated fool

Northwest Passage

45,000 years & there was
never a way through the ice
before you said you had enough pills
to kill yourself and that
you thought
it would be like a flashbulb
going off inside your head
first the radiance then
the blue dot of perfect
blindness

Crushing a Spider

pain so vast
it appears   like a sunrise
bright and hot at the center   dark
at the horizon

gut-spun nets
oak leaves snared
veined and perfect
drops of water each brilliant as
a mirror
held up to eternity

(which
    like death
can be caught
but not held)

The Wrecking Yard

after childhood life is mostly
a matter of being disassembled

an arm or finger here   a knee
there   lust wrung out and
replaced with fatigue

as you kneel and try to gather up
the pieces   you remember
yourself whole

that's the worst
torment   that image of
yourself walking out to get
the mail or admiring your
breasts in the mirror

the young do not want to hear
that all gifts are taken back
healthy and beautiful they
damage one another
while the old sleep on
dumb and content
dreaming of dead lovers   the smell of rain

  long white roads
  choked with
      dust

The Fear Closet

4 am bolt upright spine
clicking like Venetian blinds
mother dead father dead lover
dead   planet only fit for roaches
blue shapes heave
in the darkness
whispering of cancer   heart disease
and contempt as
your discarded clothing rises
up soiled puppets staggering around
the bed whispering *we don't like you we*
never have   your shoes transformed
into goblets brimming with
hatred so bitter it withers your tongue

which is worse at that hour?
that you are likely to die
or likely to end up limping down
the street pushing a rusty shopping cart
while young punks discuss
whether or not to kill you for your
rings?   eighty miles away a flame is
burning under a skillet   water is running
into a tub   gas is hissing like a pile
of copulating snakes and you have forgotten
something so important no one will   ever
forgive you

The First Church of Sex

In front of the First Church of Sex
the doctors gather to inspect
our ankles
we have clambered down cliffs
to get here   our stockings are torn
we are ashamed

above us the priests are eating
vol-au-vent pastry, empty pies,
lambs that have more bones
than carp

when we open our mouths
and close our eyes

someone sucks our lips,
pours wine down our throats
and slaps wafers
on our tongues that quiver/   and buck
like dying fish

Erased

shoes without feet to wear them
liquid snail smears on a pane of glass
the watcher being watched
(learning laughter as a foreign language)

after tests
that short silence before the doctor speaks
that says it all

you will be erased
this is no joke

leave on a light   I can no longer
sleep in a dark room
the walls are bending around me
gnawing slowly at my body
like a pack of dogs

erased?   must you repeat?

me?

            but not you, right?

never you

Nightlight

more than the mad witches in the closet
combing the snakes on their heads
or the soft lumps of
flesh under the bed that turned
and moaned constantly like bare
maple branches scraping a windowpane

more than the blue things that hung
down from the ceiling   candle wax monsters
dripping   teeth bared   clawing away
rattle rattle   like rats in
the wall

all of these were nothing   compared
to the black sheet that folded
itself around me each night
at eight

anything could come out of it

demons speaking in tongues like crazed
preachers   rusty razorblades
bent on slitting me from ear to ear
strange, thin men with melting
faces who would only speak in whispers
as they went about their gristly business

worse yet nothing might come
out because nothing was in there

nothing
had ever been in there

a child could fall into that open pit
as easily as she could fall into a well
fill herself with blankness

feast on black blood
forget to keep the pulse in her wrist
ticking

forget to breathe

Nightlight II

in the dark   a crisis of faith
drugs against the quick snuff
the long slow fall

which is the way the world
coils   all amazon and boa
on clear water with black bubbles
rising from vast caverns
where the fish have
no eyes

Travel Advisory

your past
has been buried at the crossroads
with a stake in its heart

now you can go east or west
north or south

the problem is which
to choose

river of lava?   plain of sand?
lake of salt and coyote bones?

trite useless
not worth the trip

You could go blind instead
    bloody your fingers
on stones you mistook for friendship

at the end there might be light
or even ecstasy

or . . .

but of course you always knew
it was waiting for you
that in the end
it would be something soft
something that slipped through your fingers
like fine hair

What Comes After

I did not know it would be so cold
or that such fierce winds would cantle me

cantle

a word caught between horse and candle

the sound light makes
as it rushes past

The Breakdown of Language/ The Failure of Translation

you do not want
  to know
how *(a febre)*
if (the break)

    glass splinters
(a ruptura da linguagem)
foot as if
Chinese ideo-
grammatical
  the gentlemen
long river wash
nothing seeing
the death of______

consider (sharp
break) the heel
a gaping   but *o quê?*

  what?*

**falha da tradução*

PART IV

FADO TROPICAL

Fado Tropical

O mundo do rio   the world of the river
is not the world of the bridge   not the world
of memory   *não o mundo do passado*
not the world of the past   *não o mundo da*
saudade   not the world of longing

beneath the pollen that lacquers the surface   beneath the light
that combs the water   something indeterminate
lies in wait

o que é   what is it
that swims like a fish but is not a fish
that eats bone and flesh but has no teeth
cold-blooded, intelligent
suave como uma pantera   smooth as a panther

Leia a água
read the river

translate

A Reunião / The Conference

When I entered the hall
they filled my head with birds
macaws   parrots   chachalacas

I could feel them whistling crackling
bumping into one another behind
my sinuses   the birds sang of love & death
poetry put in cages   people
who only wrote to mimic the sounds
of their own voices   rich women
who tried to buy prizes

but I wanted to hear the sounds of the
jungle   the vast humming of sap
running through ten million trees
the slither of the *cascavel muda*
the hush of a lone dugout canoe
riding the current   the silent running
of piranhas & pink dolphins
the ancient music of hot nights
drenched and burned
in the trilling of transparent frogs

How We Lost Solange

We heard there was a price on your head
that the *jagunços* were after you because
you had occupied land you did not own
insulted the colonels
and drunk *caçhaca* with handsome slim-
hipped men young enough to be your sons

they said you
had turned into a parrot
and flown into the jungle
that your legs had been eaten off
by termites
that the Kayapó found you
wrapped you in bark
made you whole again
and fed you bitter potions concocted from
dragon's blood milk of the *ila,* cat's claw, and *lanhuiqui*

they said you slept naked with the Kuikuro
Matipu Mehinako Nahukuá Suyá Trumai
Waura and Yawalapiti in a promiscuous pile
refusing to say whether you preferred
to have sex with women or men
because the distinction
made no sense

far up the Xingu, they said,
you reclined in a hammock
made of human finger bones
chewing on the blue gills of
phantom plecos and feeding your
lust with spicy stews made
from piranhas and spotted corys

they said that since you
left us you had drunk human blood

ascended above the canopy
on a jacaré skin
and spoken to gods so terrible
that not even the Aweti dared to look
you in the face

we formed a rescue team
and went in with helicopters
and tranquilizers hoping to get to you
before the *jagunços* did

but you saw us coming
in a dream
and left on a ribbon of water
and gold light   trailing your
long brown hair behind you like a
torn flag

in the note we found
tied to the thumb of your hammock
you told us we would
never find you
you wrote that you had taken
a jaguar for a lover
sifted your flesh
into the great oxbow lakes
where it rains black mud
cast off the flowered
husk of your body
and become a white orchid
floating on dark water

Notes

The Jaguars That Prowl Our Dreams: The Rio Negro, Solimões, Xingu, Javary and Tocantins are tributaries of the Amazon. The Orinoco flows through Venezuela and Colombia.

Sugar Zone: This poem contains references to the novel *A Primeira Mulher* by Miguel Sanches *Neto.*

There's No Sin South of the Equator is the English translation of the title of the song *Não existe pecado al sul do Equador* by Chico Buarque and Ruy Guerra. This poem also contains references to *Fábula Do Ribeirão do Carmo* by eighteenth century Brazilian poet Cláudio Manuel da Costa.

Along the River: This poem contains references to the novel *The Smile of the Lizard* by João Ubaldo Ribeiro.

On a Sea of Burning Roses: the title of this poem is my translation of a line from Pedro Kilkerry's poem *Sobre um mar de rosas que arde.*

Bone China: this poem contains references to *Motivo* by Cecília Meirelles.

Yansan: In the Afro-Brazilian religion Candomblé, Yansan is the goddess of wind and storms.

*The Breakdown of Language/The Failure of Translation: *falha da tradução* = failure of translation.

Fado Tropical: Fados are Portuguese songs about loss and longing. The word *"fado"* also means "fate." The first two lines of this poem were inspired by Maria Bethânia's *"O Mundo Do Rio Nao É O Mundo da Ponte Onde Eu Nasci Passa Um Rio."* The phrase *"suave como uma pantera"* is a reference to Marly de Oliveira's poem *A Suave Pantera.*

About the Author

Mary Mackey received her B.A. from Harvard and a Ph.D. in Comparative Literature from the University of Michigan. During her twenties, she lived in the rain forests of Costa Rica. Her published works include five previous collections of poetry, including *Breaking The Fever* (Marsh Hawk Press, 2006). Her poems have been praised by Wendell Berry, Jane Hirshfield, Dennis Nurkse, Ron Hansen, Dennis Schmitz, and Marge Piercy for their beauty, precision, originality, and extraordinary range. Garrison Keillor has read her poetry three times on his show *The Writer's Almanac.* Mackey is also the author of twelve novels including *The Widow's War* (Berkley Books, 2009). Her works have been translated into twelve foreign languages including Japanese, Hebrew, Russian, Greek, and Finnish. For the last twenty years she has been traveling to Brazil with her husband, Angus Wright, who writes about land reform and environmental issues.

At present she is working on a series of poems inspired by the works of Brazilian poets and novelists. Combining Portuguese and English, she creates poems that use Portuguese as incantation to evoke the lyrical space that lies at the conjunction between Portuguese and English. To contact her or sample more of her work, visit her webpage at www.marymackey.com. She can also be found on Facebook.

Steve Fellner, *The Weary World Rejoices*
Mary Mackey, *Sugar Zone*
Stephen Paul Miller, *There's Only One God and You're Not It*
Thomas Fink, *Peace Conference*
Justin Petropoulos, *Eminent Domain*
Daniel Morris, *If Not for the Courage*
Norman Finkelstein, *Inside the Ghost Factory*
Neil de la Flor, *Almost Dorothy*
Phillip Lopate, *At the End of the Day: Selected Poems and An Introductory Essay*
Sandy McIntosh, *Ernesta, in the Style of the Flamenco*
Eileen Tabios, *The Thorn Rosary: Selected Prose Poems and New (1998–2010)*
Paul Pines, *Last Call at the Tin Palace*
Corrine Robins, *Facing It: New and Selected Poems*
Edward Foster, *The Beginning of Sorrows.*
Stephen Paul Miller, *Fort Dad*
Patricia Carlin, *Quantum Jitters*
Michael Rerick, *In Ways Impossible to Fold*
Harriet Zinnes, *Light Light or the Curvature of the Earth*
Rochelle Ratner, *Ben Casey Days*
Jane Augustine, *A Woman's Guide to Mountain Climbing*
Thomas Fink, *Clarity and Other Poems*
Karin Randolph, *Either She Was*
Norman Finkelstein, *Passing Over*
Sandy McIntosh, *Forty-Nine Guaranteed Ways to Escape Death*
Eileen Tabios, *The Light Sang As It Left Your Eyes*
Claudia Carlson, *The Elephant House*
Steve Fellner, *Blind Date with Cavafy*
Basil King, *77 Beasts: Basil King's Bestiary*
Rochelle Ratner, *Balancing Acts*
Corinne Robins, *Today's Menu*
Mary Mackey, *Breaking the Fever*
Sigman Byrd, *Under the Wanderer's Star*
Edward Foster, *What He Ought To Know*
Sharon Olinka, *The Good City*
Harriet Zinnes, *Whither Nonstopping*
Sandy McIntosh, *The After-Death History of My Mother*
Eileen R. Tabios, *I Take Thee, English, for My Beloved*
Burt Kimmelman, *Somehow*
Stephen Paul Miller, *Skinny Eighth Avenue*
Jacquelyn Pope, *Watermark*
Jane Augustine, *Night Lights*
Thomas Fink, *After Taxes*
Martha King, *Imperfect Fit*
Susan Terris, *Natural Defenses*
Daniel Morris, *Bryce Passage*
Corinne Robins, *One Thousand Years*
Chard deNiord, *Sharp Golden Thorn*
Rochelle Ratner, *House and Home*
Basil King, *Mirage*
Sharon Dolin, *Serious Pink*
Madeline Tiger, *Birds of Sorrow and Joy*
Patricia Carlin, *Original Green*
Stephen Paul Miller, *The Bee Flies in May*
Edward Foster, *Mahrem: Things Men Should Do for Men*
Eileen R. Tabios, *Reproductions of the Empty Flagpole*
Harriet Zinnes, *Drawing on the Wall*
Thomas Fink, *Gossip: A Book of Poems*
Jane Augustine, *Arbor Vitae*
Sandy McIntosh, *Between Earth and Sky*
Burt Kimmelman and Fred Caruso, *The Pond at Cape May Point*